a visit to the ZOO

by Lois Vanderhoef
photographs by Gerry Swart

The baby gorilla uses his long arms to walk and run in the grass.

Here's a friendly chimpanzee. He's glad to see you!

Tiger has a beautiful striped coat.

This family of lions is called a *pride*.

The lion cubs are tired of napping.
They want to play!

When the tall giraffe wants a drink of water, she has a long way to bend.

This rhinoceros is big and strong and has two fine horns on his nose.

The largest animal in the zoo is the gigantic elephant.

It's lunchtime, and Baby Zebra is hungry for her mother's milk.

The camel will
have some hay
for *his* lunch.

The grass makes a tasty snack for a hungry antelope.

Raccoon likes to dunk her food in the water before she eats it.

The Arctic fox has a thick fur coat to keep him warm in the winter.

Polar Bear is
showing us how
tall he can stand.

Swimming is a good way for the big
brown bear to stay cool in the summer.

The ostrich is the biggest bird in the world.

Penguins can't fly, but they're good swimmers.

Flamingos stand on one leg for a long time.
Can you do that?

Good-bye, Dolphin! We'll be back soon to visit our zoo friends again.